Microsoft
Outlook

The Microsoft 365 Companion Series

Dr. Patrick Jones

OLYMPUS ACADEMY
PRESS

TABLE OF CONTENTS

THE HEART OF PRODUCTIVITY

In a world where time is often our most valuable resource, managing communication and schedules effectively is a cornerstone of success. Enter Microsoft Outlook—a tool that has been at the forefront of professional and personal productivity for decades. Far from being just an email client, Outlook is a powerhouse of features designed to streamline your day, connect you with others, and keep you organized in ways you might not even realize.

This book is your gateway to mastering Microsoft Outlook, whether you're a first-time user or someone looking to unlock its full potential. With a blend of practical advice, relatable examples, and actionable tips, you'll learn not only how to use Outlook but also how to make it work for you.

At its core, Microsoft Outlook is a communication tool—but that's just the beginning. Beyond sending and receiving emails, Outlook offers:

- **Calendar Management:** Plan and coordinate meetings with ease.
- **Task Organization:** Keep track of to-dos with integrated task lists.
- **Contact Management:** Store and access important details about colleagues, friends, and clients.
- **Integration:** Seamlessly connect with other Microsoft 365 apps like Teams, Word, and Excel.

Imagine starting your day with a tool that not only organizes your schedule but also prioritizes your tasks, helps you communicate effectively, and even reminds you of deadlines. That's the power of Outlook.

Outlook is packed with features, but let's face it—many of us only scratch the surface. Perhaps you've wondered how to:

- Tame an overflowing inbox.

- Set up rules to manage emails automatically.

- Coordinate meetings without endless email chains.

- Leverage Outlook's hidden tools to save time and reduce stress.

If any of this sounds familiar, you're in the right place. This book is designed to demystify Outlook, making its features accessible and actionable. Whether you use it at work, for school, or in your personal life, you'll find insights to help you transform how you manage your communication and time.

This book is structured to guide you through Outlook's features step by step, from basic functionality to advanced tools. Each chapter builds on the last, offering a comprehensive journey into the heart of this essential tool:

1. **What Is Microsoft Outlook?** A deep dive into Outlook's capabilities and how it integrates with the Microsoft 365 ecosystem.

2. **Why Use Microsoft Outlook?** Discover the benefits of Outlook, from its robust organization tools to its time-saving integrations.

3. **Getting Started:** Learn how to set up and customize Outlook to meet your needs.

4. **Best Practices:** Explore strategies to manage your inbox, calendar, and tasks effectively.

5. **Tips and Tricks:** Unlock hidden features and shortcuts that can revolutionize how you use Outlook.

6. **Copilot in Outlook:** Discover how AI-driven tools like Copilot can enhance productivity and simplify communication.

7. **Common Pitfalls:** Identify challenges users often face and learn how to overcome them.

8. **Episode:** Follow Sarah's relatable journey as she learns to harness Outlook to conquer her chaotic workday.

9. **Summary and Reflection:** Recap the key lessons and see how Sarah's story mirrors your own transformation.

10. **Final Thoughts:** Conclude with inspiration to explore Outlook further and embrace its role in the broader Microsoft 365 suite.

Throughout this book, you'll follow the story of Sarah, a project manager juggling countless emails, meetings, and deadlines. Like many of us, Sarah struggled to keep up until she discovered the full potential of Microsoft Outlook. From organizing her inbox to mastering calendar invites, Sarah's journey is one of growth, discovery, and newfound efficiency.

Her experiences serve as a guide, illustrating how the lessons in each chapter can be applied in real life. You'll see yourself in Sarah's challenges and find inspiration in her solutions.

One of Outlook's greatest strengths is its adaptability. It's equally valuable for:

- **Professionals:** Streamline workflows, manage teams, and stay ahead of deadlines.

- **Students:** Organize classes, assignments, and group projects.

- **Families:** Coordinate schedules, plan events, and keep everyone on the same page.

No matter your role, Outlook's features can be tailored to meet your needs.

While many tools focus on a single function, Outlook is a hub for productivity. Its ability to combine communication, scheduling, and task management in one place sets it apart. Plus, its seamless integration with the Microsoft 365 suite means you can transition effortlessly between apps, whether you're drafting an email, scheduling a meeting, or collaborating on a document.

Imagine you're preparing for a big presentation. You schedule a team meeting in Outlook, attach the draft PowerPoint file directly to the invite, and use Copilot to review the most relevant emails about the project—all without leaving the app.

Outlook is a tool with the potential to change the way you work, communicate, and stay organized. But unlocking its full power requires more than just familiarity—it takes understanding, practice, and a willingness to explore.

WHAT IS MICROSOFT OUTLOOK?

Microsoft Outlook is much more than an email client—it's a dynamic productivity hub that brings together communication, scheduling, task management, and collaboration into a single, seamless experience. For decades, Outlook has been a cornerstone of workplace efficiency, and with continuous updates and integrations in the Microsoft 365 ecosystem, it remains one of the most versatile tools for managing modern workflows.

But what exactly is Microsoft Outlook? Let's break it down into its core components, explore its features, and uncover how it connects with other Microsoft apps to create a powerful ecosystem for personal and professional success.

Outlook first emerged in 1997 as part of Microsoft Office, designed to centralize email and calendar functions. Over time, it evolved into a comprehensive tool that includes task management, contact storage, and seamless integration with Microsoft's other applications. Today, Outlook is available as:

- A desktop application for Windows and macOS.
- A web app accessible via Outlook.com or Office.com.
- A mobile app for iOS and Android devices.

With consistent updates, Outlook has adapted to meet the needs of its users, from individuals managing their personal lives to global enterprises coordinating large-scale operations.

At its heart, Outlook is designed to help you communicate, organize, and collaborate efficiently. Its primary features include:

1. **Email Management**
   - Send, receive, and organize emails with ease.
   - Create folders and categories to sort messages for quick retrieval.

- o Use filters and search functions to locate specific emails in seconds.

Example: Sarah, a project manager, uses rules to automatically sort incoming emails into project-specific folders, saving her time each morning.

2. **Calendar and Scheduling**
   - o Plan meetings and appointments with Outlook's robust calendar.
   - o View schedules in various formats, from daily agendas to monthly overviews.
   - o Send meeting invites and track RSVPs directly from the app.

Example: Sarah schedules team meetings by checking availability through the shared calendar feature, ensuring everyone can attend.

3. **Task Management**
   - o Create to-do lists and set reminders for important deadlines.
   - o Link tasks to emails or calendar events for seamless tracking.
   - o Prioritize tasks to stay focused on what matters most.

Pro Tip: Use the "My Day" view to see your calendar and tasks side by side.

4. **Contact Management**
   - o Store and manage contact information for colleagues, clients, and friends.

- o Group contacts into categories for targeted communication.
- o Integrate with other apps like Teams for instant collaboration.

Example: Sarah saves key client details in Outlook, making it easy to send personalized emails or schedule calls.

5. **Search and Organization Tools**
   - o Use advanced search to find emails, attachments, or calendar events.
   - o Organize your inbox with flags, categories, and tags.
   - o Archive old emails to keep your inbox clutter-free while retaining important information.

One of Outlook's greatest strengths is its seamless integration with other Microsoft 365 apps. This connectivity transforms Outlook from a standalone tool into a central hub for collaboration and productivity.

- **Teams:** Schedule and join Teams meetings directly from the Outlook calendar. Share emails and files in Teams chats for instant context.
- **Word and Excel:** Attach documents to emails or meeting invites, and open them directly in their respective apps for editing.
- **OneDrive:** Access and share cloud-stored files without leaving Outlook.
- **Planner:** Convert emails into tasks in Planner to streamline project management.

Example: Sarah drafts a report in Word, attaches it to an Outlook email, and shares it with her team. When feedback is needed, she schedules a

Teams meeting from the same email thread for a collaborative discussion.

Outlook's ability to centralize multiple productivity functions into one platform is one of its standout features. Instead of juggling separate apps for email, calendar, and task management, users can handle everything in one place.

Key Benefits Include:

- **Time Savings:** Access all your tools in one interface, reducing the need to switch between apps.

- **Improved Focus:** Keep emails, schedules, and tasks interconnected to maintain a clear workflow.

- **Enhanced Collaboration:** Share information effortlessly with colleagues and sync data across devices.

Outlook is available in various forms, each tailored to different user needs:

1. **Outlook for Desktop:** The most feature-rich version, ideal for power users managing complex workflows.

2. **Outlook on the Web:** Accessible through a browser, offering flexibility for users who work across devices.

3. **Outlook Mobile:** Optimized for on-the-go productivity, with a focus on quick access to emails, calendars, and tasks.

Pro Tip: Sync your accounts across all versions to ensure consistency and accessibility, no matter where you are.

In today's hybrid work environment, where teams are often spread across locations and time zones, Outlook plays a crucial role in keeping communication and schedules aligned. Its integration with cloud-based tools like OneDrive and SharePoint ensures that users can collaborate in real time, regardless of physical location.

Example: Sarah uses Outlook to schedule a virtual meeting with her global team, attach the project brief stored in OneDrive, and send reminders to ensure everyone is prepared.

While other tools focus on singular functions, Outlook excels as an all-in-one productivity solution. Its unique combination of features and integrations makes it more than just an email client—it's a comprehensive platform for managing your day.

Why Users Love Outlook:

- It's customizable, allowing you to tailor the interface and settings to your preferences.

- It's secure, offering enterprise-grade protection for emails and sensitive data.

- It's scalable, serving the needs of individuals, small businesses, and large enterprises alike.

Now that you understand what Microsoft Outlook is and how it fits into the Microsoft 365 ecosystem, the next step is exploring why you should use it.

WHY USE MICROSOFT OUTLOOK?

Microsoft Outlook has long been a staple in the world of communication and organization, but what makes it such a vital tool? Why should you consider Outlook not just as an email client but as a cornerstone of your productivity? The answer lies in its versatility, integration, and ability to transform how you manage your time, tasks, and connections.

In this chapter, we'll explore the compelling reasons to use Microsoft Outlook, showing how it adapts to diverse needs—whether you're an individual seeking efficiency or part of a global team striving for seamless collaboration.

1. Centralized Communication Hub

One of Outlook's greatest strengths is its ability to centralize communication. Rather than juggling multiple platforms, Outlook allows you to:

- Send and receive emails in a clean, organized interface.
- Access past conversations easily with its powerful search functionality.
- Manage multiple email accounts in one place, whether they're work, school, or personal accounts.

Example: Sarah manages her personal and professional emails through Outlook, enabling her to switch contexts without switching apps.

Pro Tip: Use categories and folders to organize emails, ensuring that nothing important slips through the cracks.

2. Powerful Scheduling and Calendar Features

Outlook's calendar is more than just a scheduling tool—it's your personal assistant for time management. With Outlook, you can:

- Plan meetings, appointments, and events with ease.
- View multiple calendars side by side to avoid conflicts.
- Set reminders and notifications to stay on top of deadlines.

Example: Sarah uses Outlook to schedule weekly team meetings, attaching agendas and documents directly to the calendar invite.

Why It Matters: A well-managed calendar reduces stress, keeps you on track, and ensures that you're always prepared for what's next.

3. Task and To-Do Integration

Outlook's task management features bring organization to your workflow. With integrated to-do lists, you can:

- Create tasks and set due dates to stay organized.
- Prioritize your to-do items to focus on what's most important.
- Link tasks to emails, ensuring all relevant information is in one place.

Example: After receiving an email about a project deadline, Sarah converts it into a task with one click, ensuring she doesn't forget to follow up.

Pro Tip: Use the "My Day" view to see tasks and calendar events side by side, giving you a clear picture of your priorities.

4. Seamless Collaboration and Integration

Outlook shines when it comes to collaboration, particularly in environments where teamwork is key. Its integration with the Microsoft 365 suite ensures that your work is connected, efficient, and accessible.

- **With Teams:** Schedule and join meetings directly from Outlook, or share emails in Teams chats for context.
- **With OneDrive:** Attach cloud-stored files to emails, ensuring recipients always have the latest version.
- **With Planner:** Turn emails into Planner tasks for better project management.

Example: Sarah uses Outlook to schedule a Teams meeting for her project team, attaching a draft stored in OneDrive to the invite for pre-meeting review.

Why It Matters: These integrations save time and reduce friction, allowing you to focus on collaboration instead of logistics.

5. Accessibility Across Devices

Outlook is designed to work wherever you do. Its consistent experience across desktop, web, and mobile means you can access your emails, calendar, and tasks no matter where you are.

- **Desktop App:** For power users who need advanced features.
- **Web App:** For quick access from any browser.
- **Mobile App:** For productivity on the go.

Example: Sarah reviews her schedule on her phone during her morning commute, ensuring she's prepared for the day ahead.

Pro Tip: Enable notifications on your mobile device for time-sensitive emails and meeting reminders.

6. Security and Privacy

In an era where data breaches are a constant concern, Outlook offers robust security features to protect your information.

- **Encryption:** Secure your emails and attachments with end-to-end encryption.

- **Spam Filtering:** Automatically filter out phishing attempts and junk mail.

- **Compliance:** Outlook meets industry standards for data privacy, making it a trusted choice for professionals in regulated industries.

Example: Sarah feels confident using Outlook to communicate sensitive project details, knowing her data is encrypted and secure.

Why It Matters: Strong security features give you peace of mind, allowing you to focus on your work instead of worrying about data protection.

7. Time-Saving Automation

Outlook's automation features streamline repetitive tasks, freeing up time for more meaningful work.

- **Rules:** Set up rules to automatically sort incoming emails into folders or flag messages based on specific criteria.

- **Quick Steps:** Use shortcuts to perform multi-step actions with a single click.

- **Copilot Integration:** Leverage AI to summarize emails, suggest meeting times, or prioritize your inbox.

Example: Sarah uses rules to automatically categorize project-related emails, ensuring her inbox stays organized without manual effort.

Pro Tip: Explore Copilot's capabilities for additional automation that adapts to your workflow.

8. Flexibility for Different Users

Outlook is as versatile as its users, making it suitable for:

- **Professionals:** Manage communication, schedules, and projects efficiently.
- **Students:** Organize assignments, classes, and group projects.
- **Families:** Coordinate events, track appointments, and stay connected.

Example: Sarah uses Outlook to manage her work emails during the day and switches to her family calendar in the evening to plan weekend activities.

Why It Matters: Outlook adapts to your needs, whether you're working in a high-pressure corporate environment or planning a family reunion.

9. Insights and Analytics

Outlook's integration with Microsoft Viva and other analytics tools provides insights into your productivity patterns.

- Track time spent in meetings and emails.
- Receive suggestions for improving focus time or reducing distractions.
- Analyze response patterns to understand communication effectiveness.

Example: Sarah reviews her weekly productivity insights, realizing she spends too much time in non-essential meetings. She adjusts her schedule to prioritize deep work.

Pro Tip: Use these insights to refine your workflow and achieve better work-life balance.

10. Longevity and Reliability

Microsoft Outlook has stood the test of time, continuously evolving to meet the needs of its users. Its widespread adoption and robust support make it a reliable choice for anyone looking to enhance productivity.

Why It Matters: You can count on Outlook to be there as your needs grow and change, with features and updates designed to keep you ahead.

Microsoft Outlook isn't just a tool—it's an enabler of smarter, more efficient work. By centralizing your communication, organizing your time, and integrating with the broader Microsoft 365 ecosystem, it empowers you to focus on what matters most.

GETTING STARTED WITH MICROSOFT OUTLOOK

Microsoft Outlook may seem like a simple email and calendar application on the surface, but it's brimming with features designed to enhance productivity. Whether you're new to Outlook or looking to refine how you use it, this chapter will guide you through the foundational steps of getting started. From setting up your account to customizing your workspace, you'll learn how to make Outlook work for you right from the beginning.

Step 1: Setting Up Your Account

To start using Outlook, you'll first need to set up your account. Outlook supports various email services, including Microsoft 365, Gmail, Yahoo, and Exchange, making it a versatile choice for managing multiple accounts.

- **On Desktop:**
    1. Open the Outlook application.
    2. On the welcome screen, click Add Account.
    3. Enter your email address and password, and follow the prompts to configure settings.

- **On Mobile:**
    1. Download the Outlook app from the App Store (iOS) or Google Play Store (Android).
    2. Open the app and sign in with your email credentials.

Pro Tip: Use the same account across devices to keep your data synced.

Example: Sarah uses her Microsoft 365 work account on her desktop and mobile device, ensuring she can access her emails and calendar no matter where she is.

Step 2: Exploring the Interface

Outlook's interface is designed for efficiency, but understanding its layout is key to using it effectively.

- **The Ribbon:** At the top, the ribbon contains commands for common tasks like sending emails, creating calendar events, and managing contacts.

- **Navigation Pane:** On the left, this pane lets you switch between Mail, Calendar, Tasks, and Contacts.

- **Reading Pane:** This is where you preview the content of emails without opening them fully.

- **Folders:** Found on the left side of the Mail view, folders help you organize your inbox.

Pro Tip: Customize the ribbon to include your most-used commands for quicker access.

Example: Sarah adds the "New Meeting" and "Search" commands to her ribbon, making it easier to schedule events and find emails quickly.

Step 3: Setting Up Your Inbox

Outlook's email tools go beyond just reading and sending messages. Setting up your inbox correctly can save you time and reduce stress.

- **Create Folders:** Organize your emails into folders based on projects, clients, or categories.

- **Use Rules:** Set up rules to automatically sort incoming emails into specific folders.

o Example: Emails from your manager go directly into a "Priority" folder.

- **Flag Important Emails:** Use flags to mark emails that require follow-up.

Pro Tip: Turn on "Focused Inbox" to automatically separate important emails from less critical ones.

Example: Sarah uses rules to filter meeting invites into a dedicated folder, keeping her primary inbox clear.

Step 4: Managing Your Calendar

Outlook's calendar is a powerful tool for managing your time and staying organized. Here's how to get started:

- **Adding Events:**
  o Click "New Event" and enter details like date, time, and location.
  o Add notes or attachments for context.

- **Inviting Others:**
  o Add attendees to your event and send invitations directly from the calendar.
  o Use "Scheduling Assistant" to find the best time for everyone.

- **Setting Reminders:**
  o Configure reminders to ensure you're prepared for meetings or tasks.

Pro Tip: Use color categories to differentiate personal, work, and team events at a glance.

Example: Sarah blocks time for deep work by creating recurring "Focus Time" events on her calendar.

Step 5: Customizing Outlook to Fit Your Needs

Outlook is highly customizable, allowing you to tailor its features to your preferences.

- **Themes:** Change the color scheme to make the interface visually appealing.
- **Quick Steps:** Automate multi-step tasks, such as forwarding emails with pre-written responses.
- **Notifications:** Configure email and calendar alerts to stay informed without being overwhelmed.

Pro Tip: If you're working across time zones, enable the dual-time zone feature in the calendar settings to simplify scheduling.

Example: Sarah creates a Quick Step to forward client feedback emails to her team with a pre-written template, saving her time each day.

Step 6: Syncing with Other Devices and Apps

Outlook's seamless syncing capabilities ensure that your data is consistent across devices and apps.

- **Mobile Sync:** Install the Outlook app on your phone to access emails, calendars, and tasks on the go.
- **Integration with Microsoft 365 Apps:**
  - Link tasks with Microsoft To-Do for comprehensive task management.
  - Schedule Teams meetings directly from your Outlook calendar.

Pro Tip: Use OneDrive to attach files to emails, ensuring recipients always have the most up-to-date version.

Example: Sarah reviews her calendar on her mobile app during her commute, preparing for the day ahead.

Step 7: Exploring Additional Features

Outlook is packed with features that go beyond the basics. As you become more comfortable, explore these advanced tools:

- **Search:** Use keywords, filters, and tags to find specific emails or calendar events quickly.

- **Shared Calendars:** Collaborate with your team by sharing calendars for better coordination.

- **Contact Groups:** Create groups for frequent email recipients, such as your project team or family members.

Pro Tip: Use Copilot (covered in detail in a later chapter) to automate tasks, prioritize emails, and summarize complex threads.

Example: Sarah creates a shared calendar for her project team, making it easy to track deadlines and milestones.

Step 8: Testing and Refining Your Setup

After setting up Outlook, spend some time testing its features to ensure everything is working smoothly.

- **Check Email Rules:** Make sure your rules sort emails as intended.

- **Preview the Calendar:** Verify that events and reminders are set up correctly.

- **Experiment with Settings:** Adjust preferences like notification alerts to suit your workflow.

Pro Tip: Schedule a weekly review to declutter your inbox and update tasks or calendar events.

Example: Sarah spends 15 minutes every Friday organizing her inbox and updating her task list for the following week.

Congratulations! You've taken the first steps toward mastering Microsoft Outlook. With your account set up and your workspace customized, you're now ready to dive deeper into strategies for optimizing your productivity.

BEST PRACTICES FOR USING MICROSOFT OUTLOOK

Microsoft Outlook is a powerful tool, but to truly harness its potential, you need to adopt strategies that streamline your workflow and maximize productivity. This chapter is your guide to mastering Outlook with proven best practices for managing emails, calendars, and tasks efficiently. By implementing these techniques, you'll save time, stay organized, and reduce stress in your daily routines.

1. Tame Your Inbox with Rules and Organization

The Practice:
Set up a system to sort and prioritize emails automatically. A cluttered inbox can be overwhelming, but with a few simple steps, you can keep it under control.

- **Create Folders and Categories:** Organize emails by topic, project, or priority.

- **Set Up Rules:** Automatically route emails to specific folders based on criteria like sender or subject line.

  - **Example:** Sarah set a rule to direct all emails from her manager into a "High Priority" folder.

- **Flag Important Emails:** Use flags to highlight messages that require follow-up.

Pro Tip: Dedicate a specific time each day to process emails rather than responding to them as they arrive.

2. Use the Focused Inbox Feature

The Practice:
Enable Outlook's "Focused Inbox" to separate important messages from less critical ones.

- **Why It Helps:** Focused Inbox highlights emails from frequent contacts and those with urgent subjects, keeping distractions to a minimum.

- **How to Enable It:** Go to your Inbox settings and turn on Focused Inbox.

Example: Sarah noticed that turning on Focused Inbox helped her prioritize client emails over newsletters and updates.

Pro Tip: Review the "Other" tab periodically to ensure you don't miss anything valuable.

3. Master Your Calendar

The Practice:
Use Outlook's calendar features to stay on top of your schedule and manage your time effectively.

- **Color Code Events:** Assign colors to differentiate between personal, work, and team events.

- **Set Reminders:** Configure alerts to ensure you're prepared for meetings and deadlines.

- **Use Scheduling Assistant:** Simplify meeting coordination by finding times that work for all attendees.

Example: Sarah uses color-coded categories to visualize her week—blue for meetings, green for deadlines, and orange for personal appointments.

Pro Tip: Block off time for focused work by scheduling it as a calendar event to avoid interruptions.

4. Optimize Task Management

The Practice:
Leverage Outlook's task management features to track and prioritize your to-do list.

- **Create Tasks from Emails:** Drag emails into the Tasks pane to turn them into actionable items.
- **Prioritize Tasks:** Use categories or flags to indicate urgency.
- **Integrate with To-Do:** Sync your tasks with Microsoft To-Do for a seamless experience across devices.

Example: Sarah converts her action items from emails into tasks with deadlines, ensuring she stays on track.

Pro Tip: Review your task list daily and adjust priorities as needed.

5. Reduce Meeting Fatigue with Smart Scheduling

The Practice:
Plan meetings effectively to respect everyone's time and increase productivity.

- **Set an Agenda:** Include a clear agenda in the meeting invite so attendees can prepare.
- **Use Shorter Meeting Blocks:** Schedule 25- or 50-minute meetings to allow time for transitions.
- **Schedule Recurring Events Wisely:** Regularly evaluate recurring meetings to ensure they're still necessary.

Example: Sarah shifted her weekly team meeting from 60 minutes to 45 minutes, making it more focused and effective.

Pro Tip: Use the "Propose New Time" feature to adjust meetings without endless email threads.

6. Use Quick Steps for Multi-Step Actions

The Practice:
Quick Steps automate repetitive tasks, saving you valuable time.

- **Set Up Quick Steps:** Navigate to the Quick Steps menu and create shortcuts for tasks like forwarding emails or moving messages to folders.

    o **Example:** Sarah created a Quick Step to archive completed emails with one click.

Pro Tip: Experiment with custom Quick Steps to tailor them to your workflow.

7. Take Advantage of Search and Filters

The Practice:
Outlook's search functionality is a powerful tool for finding emails, calendar events, and tasks quickly.

- **Use Search Operators:** Search for emails using keywords, dates, or senders.

    o Example: "from:John subject:report" will find all emails from John with "report" in the subject line.

- **Apply Filters:** Narrow down search results by unread emails, flagged messages, or attachments.

Pro Tip: Save frequent searches for quick access in the future.

8. Collaborate Seamlessly Across Teams

The Practice:
Outlook integrates with other Microsoft 365 tools to enhance collaboration.

- **Share Calendars:** Let team members view your availability and schedule meetings efficiently.

- **Use Teams Integration:** Schedule and join Teams meetings directly from Outlook.

- **Link with OneDrive:** Attach and share files via OneDrive to ensure recipients always have the latest version.

Example: Sarah shares her calendar with her team, allowing them to schedule collaborative sessions without back-and-forth emails.

Pro Tip: Use shared mailboxes for group communication to keep everyone aligned.

9. Customize Your Notifications

The Practice:
Set up notifications strategically to avoid interruptions while staying informed.

- **Enable Notifications for Key Events:** Configure alerts for calendar events and flagged emails.

- **Turn Off Non-Essential Alerts:** Reduce distractions by disabling notifications for newsletters or less critical emails.

Example: Sarah adjusted her notifications to focus only on meeting reminders and flagged messages.

Pro Tip: Use Do Not Disturb settings during deep work sessions to maintain focus.

10. Maintain Security and Privacy

The Practice:
Protect your data by using Outlook's built-in security features.

- **Enable Encryption:** Secure sensitive emails with end-to-end encryption.

- **Use Strong Passwords:** Ensure your Outlook account is protected with a robust password or multi-factor authentication.

- **Be Cautious with Links and Attachments:** Avoid phishing scams by verifying the sender before clicking.

Pro Tip: Regularly review your account activity to ensure there's no unauthorized access.

By adopting these best practices, you'll unlock the full potential of Microsoft Outlook, transforming it from a basic tool into a productivity powerhouse.

TIPS AND TRICKS FOR MICROSOFT OUTLOOK

Microsoft Outlook is filled with features that can save you time, streamline your workflow, and make managing your communication and schedule easier than ever. Beyond its core functionality, Outlook offers advanced tools and shortcuts that even experienced users may not know about. In this chapter, we'll explore practical tips and tricks that will help you take your Outlook skills to the next level.

1. Schedule Emails to Send Later

The Tip: Use the delay send feature to schedule emails for future delivery.

- **How to Do It:**
    - o Compose your email.
    - o Click the Options tab and select Delay Delivery.
    - o Choose the date and time you want the email to be sent.

Example: Sarah drafts client updates in the evening but schedules them to send the following morning during work hours.

Pro Tip: Use this feature to avoid sending emails outside of professional hours.

2. Customize the Reading Pane

The Tip: Adjust the reading pane settings to preview emails without fully opening them.

- **How to Customize:**
    - o Go to View > Reading Pane and choose Right, Bottom, or Off based on your preference.

Pro Tip: Turn on the "Mark as Read" setting to automatically mark emails as read when viewed in the reading pane.

3. Create Color-Coded Categories

The Tip: Use categories to visually organize emails, calendar events, and tasks.

- **How to Set It Up:**
    - Right-click an email or event and select Categorize to assign a color-coded label.
- **Example Categories:**
    - Red for urgent tasks.
    - Blue for personal items.
    - Green for team projects.

Example: Sarah categorizes her calendar events to see at a glance which meetings are client-focused versus internal.

4. Use Search Folders for Quick Access

The Tip: Create search folders to group specific emails automatically.

- **How to Set It Up:**
    - Go to Folder > New Search Folder and define criteria, such as flagged emails or messages from a specific person.

Example: Sarah creates a search folder for all emails with "deadline" in the subject line to track time-sensitive tasks.

5. Automate with Quick Steps

The Tip: Streamline repetitive actions with Quick Steps, automating tasks like forwarding emails or moving messages to folders.

- **How to Set It Up:**
    - Go to the Home tab and click Quick Steps, then New Quick Step.
    - Choose an action, such as "Move to Folder," and assign it a name and shortcut.

Pro Tip: Combine multiple actions into one Quick Step for maximum efficiency.

6. Leverage Rules for Inbox Management

The Tip: Automate your inbox by creating rules to handle incoming emails.

- **Examples of Rules:**
    - Move newsletters to a "Subscriptions" folder.
    - Flag emails from your manager automatically.
    - Delete emails from certain senders.

How to Set It Up:

- Right-click an email, select Rules > Create Rule, and define your criteria.

Example: Sarah uses rules to filter client emails into project-specific folders, keeping her inbox clutter-free.

7. Integrate Copilot for Smarter Workflows

The Tip: Let Microsoft Copilot handle complex tasks, such as summarizing long email threads or suggesting optimal meeting times.

- **Examples of Copilot Use:**

- Summarizing a week's worth of emails into actionable insights.

- Drafting replies based on email context.

- Highlighting key points in meeting requests or email chains.

Pro Tip: Use clear prompts to guide Copilot for the best results.

8. Sync with Other Microsoft Apps

The Tip: Extend Outlook's capabilities by syncing it with other Microsoft 365 tools.

- **Examples of Integrations:**

  - **Teams:** Schedule and join meetings directly from Outlook.

  - **To-Do:** Sync tasks and reminders seamlessly.

  - **OneDrive:** Attach and share cloud-stored files.

Example: Sarah links her Outlook tasks with To-Do, ensuring she never misses an important deadline.

9. Optimize Notifications for Focus

The Tip: Customize notifications to stay informed without constant interruptions.

- **How to Customize:**

  - Go to File > Options > Mail and adjust notification settings.

  - Disable alerts for non-essential folders or categories.

Pro Tip: Use Focus Assist (on Windows) to suppress Outlook notifications during deep work sessions.

These tips and tricks are just the beginning of what you can achieve with Microsoft Outlook. By incorporating even a few of these strategies, you'll find your workflow smoother, your time better managed, and your productivity soaring.

YOUR AI-POWERED PRODUCTIVITY PARTNER

Imagine having an assistant who can help you draft emails, summarize lengthy threads, prioritize your inbox, and even suggest meeting times—all without breaking a sweat. That's the power of Microsoft Copilot in Outlook. This AI-driven tool is transforming the way we communicate and manage our work, making it easier to stay organized and productive.

In this chapter, we'll dive into what Copilot is, how it integrates with Outlook, and practical ways to use it to save time and simplify your day.

Microsoft Copilot is an artificial intelligence tool embedded within Microsoft 365 apps, including Outlook. It leverages advanced AI models and natural language processing to assist with everyday tasks, turning complex processes into simple, actionable steps.

In Outlook, Copilot works alongside you to:

- Summarize email threads and extract key points.
- Draft responses based on context and tone.
- Prioritize your inbox by highlighting critical messages.
- Schedule meetings efficiently by analyzing availability.

Pro Tip: Think of Copilot as a collaborator—it's here to enhance your productivity, not replace your input or decision-making.

Using Copilot in Outlook is simple. Look for the Copilot icon (a small assistant or AI symbol) in your toolbar or message interface. Once enabled, you can interact with Copilot via text prompts or by selecting predefined tasks.

Examples of Commands You Can Give Copilot:

- "Summarize this email thread in three points."

- "Draft a reply expressing interest in the proposal but asking for more details."
- "Schedule a 30-minute meeting with John and Emma next week."

Pro Tip: Be specific with your prompts to get the most relevant results.

Key Features of Copilot in Outlook

1. **Email Summarization**
   - **What It Does:** Copilot condenses lengthy email threads into concise summaries, highlighting key points and action items.
   - **How It Helps:** Saves time by eliminating the need to read through every message in a chain.
   - **Example:** Sarah uses Copilot to quickly understand the main takeaways from a week-long client email exchange.

Pro Tip: Use this feature when you're catching up after time away or managing high volumes of email.

2. **Drafting Responses**
   - **What It Does:** Copilot drafts email replies based on the context of the conversation. You can customize tone and content before sending.
   - **How It Helps:** Reduces the time spent crafting responses while maintaining professionalism.
   - **Example:** When Sarah receives a project inquiry, Copilot drafts a polite reply acknowledging the email and requesting additional details.

Pro Tip: Review drafts thoroughly to ensure they align with your voice and intent.

3. **Inbox Prioritization**

   o **What It Does:** Copilot scans your inbox to identify high-priority messages and suggests actions.

   o **How It Helps:** Keeps you focused on what matters most, especially during busy periods.

   o **Example:** Copilot highlights an email marked as urgent from Sarah's manager, ensuring she addresses it promptly.

Pro Tip: Combine this feature with Outlook's Focused Inbox for maximum efficiency.

4. **Meeting Scheduling**

   o **What It Does:** Copilot analyzes calendars to find the best meeting times for participants and sends invites automatically.

   o **How It Helps:** Simplifies the back-and-forth of scheduling, saving time for everyone involved.

   o **Example:** Sarah uses Copilot to schedule a team check-in, ensuring availability across time zones.

Pro Tip: Pair this feature with Outlook's Scheduling Assistant for greater accuracy.

5. **Follow-Up Reminders**

   o **What It Does:** Copilot tracks your commitments and suggests follow-ups for unanswered emails or pending tasks.

   o **How It Helps:** Prevents important items from slipping through the cracks.

o **Example:** Copilot reminds Sarah to follow up on an email she sent to a client three days ago.

Pro Tip: Use this feature to stay proactive in your communication.

Copilot isn't just about individual productivity—it also strengthens teamwork by streamlining communication and coordination.

- **Collaborative Drafting:** Copilot can help draft group emails or meeting summaries, saving time for the entire team.
- **Shared Insights:** Use Copilot to analyze responses from shared inboxes and highlight trends or action items.
- **Integrated Tools:** Seamlessly connect Copilot with Teams and SharePoint to share insights and updates.

Example: Sarah uses Copilot to summarize a project status email and shares the summary in a Teams channel for her colleagues to review.

Advanced Copilot Features to Explore

1. **Customizable Prompts:** Adjust prompts to match your specific needs, such as "Write a formal response" or "Summarize with bullet points."
2. **Data-Driven Suggestions:** Use Copilot to identify recurring themes in email feedback or survey responses.
3. **Time Zone Awareness:** Copilot accounts for time zones when scheduling meetings, ensuring inclusivity for global teams.

Pro Tip: Experiment with different types of prompts to discover new ways Copilot can assist you.

Tips for Getting the Most Out of Copilot

- **Start Small:** Use Copilot for basic tasks like drafting emails or summarizing threads before diving into advanced features.

- **Be Specific:** Provide clear and detailed prompts to get the best results.

- **Review Output:** Always review Copilot's suggestions to ensure accuracy and alignment with your goals.

- **Stay Updated:** Keep an eye on Microsoft's updates to Copilot, as new features are added regularly.

As AI continues to evolve, Copilot will only become more powerful and intuitive. Future updates may include deeper integration with other apps, enhanced natural language understanding, and even predictive suggestions based on your habits and preferences.

Looking Ahead: Copilot is a glimpse into the future of productivity, where AI doesn't just assist—it amplifies your ability to work smarter.

Now that you've learned about Copilot's capabilities in Outlook, it's time to see it in action.

COMMON PITFALLS AND HOW TO AVOID THEM

Microsoft Outlook is an incredible tool, but like any software, its effectiveness depends on how you use it. Missteps in setup, organization, or daily use can lead to inefficiency, missed communications, or even data loss. The good news? These pitfalls are avoidable once you know what to watch for.

This chapter identifies common mistakes Outlook users make and provides actionable strategies to overcome them. By addressing these challenges head-on, you'll unlock the full potential of Outlook while sidestepping unnecessary frustrations.

1. Letting Your Inbox Become Overwhelmed

The Pitfall:
A cluttered inbox can make it hard to find important messages and prioritize your work.

Why It Happens:
Many users rely solely on manual organization or neglect their inbox altogether.

How to Avoid It:

- **Use Rules:** Automatically sort emails into folders based on sender, subject, or keywords.

- **Archive Old Emails:** Move older, less critical emails to an archive folder to keep your inbox tidy.

- **Daily Inbox Zero:** Dedicate a few minutes daily to clear out your inbox, respond to urgent messages, and file less critical ones.

Example: Sarah struggled with an overflowing inbox until she set up rules to automatically sort client emails into dedicated folders.

Pro Tip: Combine Outlook's Focused Inbox with manual sorting for maximum clarity.

2. Neglecting Calendar Management

The Pitfall:
Missing meetings or double-booking yourself due to poor calendar habits.

Why It Happens:
Failing to review your schedule regularly or forgetting to update events can lead to chaos.

How to Avoid It:

- **Set Calendar Alerts:** Enable reminders for all important meetings.
- **Block Focus Time:** Schedule time for deep work to prevent interruptions.
- **Sync Across Devices:** Ensure your calendar updates in real time on desktop, mobile, and web.

Example: Sarah avoided double bookings by regularly checking her shared team calendar for conflicts before accepting new invites.

Pro Tip: Use color-coded categories to differentiate between personal, team, and client meetings.

3. Relying on Memory for Tasks

The Pitfall:
Forgetting tasks or deadlines because you don't record them systematically.

Why It Happens:
Relying solely on memory or scattered notes leads to dropped balls.

How to Avoid It:

- **Use Tasks in Outlook:** Turn emails into tasks with deadlines and priorities.

- **Integrate with To-Do:** Sync tasks between Outlook and Microsoft To-Do for a unified list.

- **Review Regularly:** Check your task list daily to stay on top of commitments.

Example: Sarah made a habit of converting action items from emails into tasks, ensuring nothing slipped through the cracks.

4. Ignoring Security Features

The Pitfall:
Leaving your account vulnerable to phishing attacks or unauthorized access.

Why It Happens:
Users often underestimate the importance of email security.

How to Avoid It:

- **Enable Multi-Factor Authentication (MFA):** Add an extra layer of security to your account.

- **Be Cautious with Links and Attachments:** Verify senders before clicking links or downloading files.

- **Use Encryption:** Secure sensitive emails with built-in encryption features.

Example: Sarah avoided a phishing scam by carefully examining a suspicious email link before clicking.

Pro Tip: Regularly update your password and monitor account activity for unusual behavior.

5. Failing to Customize Notifications

The Pitfall:
Constant notifications lead to distraction and decreased productivity.

Why It Happens:
Default notification settings often include alerts for every incoming email or calendar event.

How to Avoid It:

- **Turn Off Non-Essential Alerts:** Disable notifications for newsletters or low-priority folders.

- **Enable Focus Assist:** Use Windows' Focus Assist feature to block notifications during deep work sessions.

- **Customize Calendar Alerts:** Set reminders only for critical meetings or deadlines.

Example: Sarah reduced distractions by silencing non-essential notifications and checking her email only at scheduled times.

6. Overlooking Search and Organization Tools

The Pitfall:
Wasting time manually searching for emails, attachments, or events.

Why It Happens:
Many users don't take advantage of Outlook's robust search and filtering options.

How to Avoid It:

- **Use Search Operators:** Search by keywords, sender, or date to narrow results.

- **Save Frequent Searches:** Save commonly used search queries for quick access.

- **Leverage Filters:** Sort emails by unread, flagged, or with attachments.

Example: Sarah used filters to quickly locate all unread emails from her manager within the past week.

Pro Tip: Use search folders to group emails that meet specific criteria, like flagged items or messages with attachments.

7. Not Taking Advantage of Automation

The Pitfall:
Manually performing repetitive tasks that could be automated.

Why It Happens:
Users may not be aware of Outlook's automation capabilities.

How to Avoid It:

- **Set Up Quick Steps:** Automate multi-step processes like forwarding emails or filing messages.

- **Utilize Copilot:** Leverage AI for drafting responses, summarizing threads, and prioritizing tasks.

Example: Sarah created Quick Steps to forward emails to her team and mark them as read simultaneously.

8. Skipping Updates and New Features

The Pitfall:
Using outdated features or missing out on new tools that could improve productivity.

Why It Happens:
Some users stick to familiar workflows and avoid exploring updates.

How to Avoid It:

- **Stay Updated:** Regularly install updates to access the latest features and security patches.

- **Explore New Tools:** Take time to learn about added functionalities, such as Copilot or enhanced integrations.

- **Follow Outlook Blogs:** Stay informed about new features through Microsoft's official resources.

Example: Sarah improved her workflow by adopting Copilot to summarize long email threads.

9. Mismanaging Shared Resources

The Pitfall:
Confusion over shared calendars or mailboxes due to lack of coordination.

Why It Happens:
Poor communication or unclear roles can lead to overlapping schedules or missed messages.

How to Avoid It:

- **Assign Roles:** Clarify who manages shared resources.

- **Set Permissions:** Restrict editing rights to prevent accidental changes.

- **Communicate Changes:** Notify team members about updates to shared calendars or folders.

Example: Sarah ensured smooth collaboration by setting clear permissions for her team's shared mailbox.

10. Ignoring Accessibility Features

The Pitfall:
Overlooking accessibility options that could improve user experience for all team members.

Why It Happens:

Users often don't realize Outlook includes robust accessibility tools.

How to Avoid It:

- **Use Accessible Themes:** Choose high-contrast themes for better visibility.

- **Enable Screen Reader Support:** Assist visually impaired team members with text-to-speech features.

- **Optimize Email Design:** Use clear fonts and avoid excessive formatting.

Pro Tip: Always test emails and events for accessibility before sending.

Avoiding these common pitfalls will help you use Microsoft Outlook more effectively, saving time and reducing stress.

SARAH'S OUTLOOK TRANSFORMATION

The soft chime of Sarah's laptop broke the quiet of her early morning routine. As she settled into her office chair, a sense of unease crept in—her inbox was already overflowing, her calendar dotted with back-to-back meetings, and her task list seemed endless. "How am I going to manage all this?" she muttered to herself, staring at the chaos on her screen.

Sarah had always prided herself on being organized, but as her responsibilities grew, so did the demands on her time. Outlook, a tool she'd used for years, had become more of a digital dumping ground than a productivity partner. She knew it was time to rethink her approach.

Sarah's first challenge of the day was tackling her inbox. Hundreds of unread emails stared back at her, a mix of client requests, project updates, and newsletter subscriptions she never quite got around to unsubscribing from. Each email felt like a small demand, pulling her in different directions.

She spent the next hour sorting through messages manually, trying to identify which ones required immediate attention. "There has to be a better way," she thought as she flagged another email.

After her third meeting of the morning—a disorganized affair where half the attendees hadn't even opened the agenda—Sarah realized she needed help. She reached out to a colleague known for her uncanny ability to manage her workload seamlessly.

"Have you tried using more of Outlook's features?" her colleague, Jessica, asked.

Sarah admitted she was only using the basics: email, a few calendar events, and an occasional task. Jessica smiled and opened her laptop.

"Outlook can do so much more," she explained. "Let me show you how I organize my day."

Jessica demonstrated how to create rules that automatically sorted incoming emails into folders.

"For example," she said, "I have a rule that sends all emails from my manager directly to a 'Priority' folder."

Jessica also showed Sarah how to use Quick Steps to automate repetitive tasks. "You can create a Quick Step to archive emails with one click," she explained.

Sarah spent the next hour setting up her own system. She created folders for clients, projects, and newsletters. Using rules, she automated her inbox so that each new email went to the right place.

By the time she finished, her inbox felt manageable for the first time in months.

Next, Jessica walked Sarah through some best practices for managing her calendar.

"Color coding is a game-changer," Jessica said. "I use blue for client meetings, green for personal events, and yellow for focus time."

Sarah quickly adopted this system, assigning colors to her events and blocking off two hours of "Focus Time" each day to tackle her most important tasks.

Jessica also showed her how to use the Scheduling Assistant to plan meetings efficiently. "It saves so much time," she said, "especially when coordinating with large teams."

Jessica introduced Sarah to the power of turning emails into tasks.

"Instead of letting action items get buried in your inbox, drag them into the Tasks pane and set deadlines," she explained.

Sarah practiced by converting an email about a client proposal into a task with a reminder. She then synced her tasks with Microsoft To-Do, giving her a clear picture of her priorities across devices.

As a final tip, Jessica demonstrated how to use Microsoft Copilot in Outlook.

"Watch this," she said, pulling up a lengthy email thread. She typed, "Summarize this thread" into Copilot, and within seconds, a concise summary appeared.

"You can also ask Copilot to draft email replies or suggest meeting times," Jessica added.

Sarah was amazed. She used Copilot to prioritize her inbox, draft a follow-up email to a client, and even schedule her next team meeting.

"This is going to save me so much time," she said with a grin.

By the end of the day, Sarah's inbox was organized, her calendar was streamlined, and her task list was actionable. She felt a sense of control she hadn't experienced in months.

As she shut down her laptop, she reflected on the changes she'd made. Outlook, once a source of stress, had become her greatest ally.

"I can finally focus on what really matters," she thought, smiling.

Sarah's story is a testament to the power of Outlook when used to its full potential. By implementing the features and strategies discussed in this book, you too can transform chaos into clarity, freeing up time and energy for what truly matters.

TRANSFORMING PRODUCTIVITY WITH MICROSOFT OUTLOOK

As we conclude this exploration of Microsoft Outlook, let's take a moment to summarize the key insights you've gained and reflect on how Sarah's journey mirrors the transformation you're now equipped to achieve. Outlook is far more than just an email tool—it's a comprehensive platform for communication, scheduling, task management, and collaboration. By leveraging its full potential, you can reclaim your time, boost your efficiency, and stay ahead of the demands of modern life.

1. **Introduction to Outlook:**
   We began by understanding Outlook's role as the central hub of the Microsoft 365 ecosystem. From email to calendar, tasks to contacts, Outlook integrates seamlessly with other tools to streamline your workflow.

2. **What Is Microsoft Outlook?:**
   This chapter explored the many features of Outlook, from its intuitive email management to its robust calendar capabilities, task organization, and integration with apps like Teams and OneDrive.

3. **Why Use Microsoft Outlook?:**
   You discovered how Outlook enhances productivity by centralizing essential functions, saving time, and fostering collaboration.

4. **Getting Started with Outlook:**
   We walked through the setup process, customizing the interface, organizing your inbox, and syncing across devices to create a foundation for success.

5. **Best Practices for Outlook:**
   From inbox zero to smart scheduling, this chapter introduced strategies to help you work smarter, not harder.

6. **Tips and Tricks:**
   You uncovered shortcuts and hidden features—like Quick Steps and Copilot—that can elevate your Outlook experience.

7. **Copilot in Outlook:**
   AI-powered Copilot was a game-changer, offering tools to summarize email threads, draft replies, prioritize messages, and schedule meetings effortlessly.

8. **Common Pitfalls and How to Avoid Them:**
   We addressed challenges like inbox overload, poor calendar management, and missed security features, equipping you with practical solutions to overcome these obstacles.

9. **Episode: Sarah's Outlook Transformation:**
   Through Sarah's relatable story, you saw how mastering Outlook's tools can turn disorganization into productivity, making complex workflows manageable and efficient.

Reflection on Sarah's Journey

Sarah's story resonates because it's a journey many of us can relate to. Like Sarah, you may have started with an overwhelming inbox, a chaotic calendar, and a feeling that you could be doing more with your time. But just as Sarah discovered, the solution lies in rethinking how you use the tools at your disposal.

- **From Overwhelmed to Organized:** Sarah's first breakthrough came when she automated her inbox with rules and folders, a reminder that small changes can lead to big results.

- **Embracing Collaboration:** By learning to manage her calendar and use tools like Scheduling Assistant, Sarah improved not only her own productivity but also her team's efficiency.

- **Harnessing the Power of AI:** Copilot's ability to summarize, prioritize, and streamline workflows showed Sarah—and you—that technology can amplify human effort.

- **Focusing on What Matters:** With her tasks organized and distractions minimized, Sarah could focus on high-impact work, illustrating the ultimate goal of productivity tools.

Sarah's journey reflects your own as you progress through this book. Every tip, trick, and feature you've learned is a step toward greater mastery of Outlook and, more importantly, greater control over your time and energy.

Microsoft Outlook isn't just about managing emails or calendars—it's about empowering you to work smarter, communicate more effectively, and stay organized in a demanding world. Each chapter of this book has been designed to build your confidence and capabilities, transforming Outlook from a tool you use occasionally into a trusted partner in your daily life.

While this book has focused on Outlook, it's just one part of the larger Microsoft 365 ecosystem. The lessons you've learned here—about automation, organization, and leveraging AI—apply across tools like Teams, SharePoint, and OneDrive.

Consider exploring:

- **Microsoft Teams:** Revolutionize communication and teamwork.

- **SharePoint:** Manage and share content across your organization.

- **Copilot Across Microsoft 365:** Discover how AI can enhance other apps in the suite.

Your Next Steps:

- Reflect on what you've learned and identify specific areas where you can implement these tools in your workflow.

- Experiment with the advanced features of Outlook to uncover new efficiencies.

- Continue your journey with other books in the *Microsoft 365 Companion Series* to deepen your mastery of the ecosystem.

Sarah's transformation is a reminder that change is possible for anyone willing to learn and adapt. By taking the time to understand and apply the strategies outlined in this book, you've equipped yourself with the tools to thrive in an increasingly connected and complex world.

The journey doesn't end here—this is just the beginning. With Microsoft Outlook as your ally, the future of your productivity is brighter than ever.

Let's move forward together, exploring new tools, embracing new challenges, and achieving new heights. The possibilities are endless!

UNLOCKING YOUR POTENTIAL WITH MICROSOFT OUTLOOK

As we reach the end of this book, take a moment to reflect on how far you've come. You've explored Microsoft Outlook not just as an email client but as a transformative tool for communication, organization, and productivity. Outlook is more than a resource—it's a gateway to working smarter, staying connected, and achieving more with your time.

But this isn't the end of your journey; it's the beginning. The tools and strategies you've learned here are stepping stones toward a greater mastery of not just Outlook but the entire Microsoft 365 ecosystem.

Outlook is a tool designed to adapt to your needs. Whether you're managing a team, coordinating personal commitments, or tackling complex projects, it provides the framework to simplify and streamline your day.

Think about how you now approach:

- **Emails:** No longer overwhelming, they're sorted, prioritized, and actionable.

- **Schedules:** Your calendar isn't just a list of meetings; it's a reflection of your goals and priorities.

- **Tasks:** You're no longer relying on memory; every to-do is tracked and manageable.

Like Sarah, you've discovered that mastering Outlook is less about learning every feature and more about using the right ones to empower your unique workflow.

While Outlook is a powerful tool on its own, its true strength lies in its connection to the broader Microsoft 365 suite. The integration between apps creates a seamless experience, enabling you to:

- Schedule meetings in Teams directly from your Outlook calendar.

- Share files from OneDrive without leaving your inbox.

- Sync tasks across Outlook and Microsoft To-Do.

- Collaborate on projects through SharePoint and Planner.

This interconnected ecosystem allows you to work fluidly, reducing the friction between tasks and focusing on what matters most.

Imagine drafting an email in Outlook, attaching a document stored in OneDrive, scheduling a review meeting in Teams, and adding follow-up tasks in Planner—all without missing a beat.

The world of Microsoft 365 is vast, and there's always more to learn. Outlook is just the beginning. By continuing to explore the tools available to you, you'll uncover new ways to work efficiently and stay ahead in a fast-paced world.

- **Microsoft Teams:** Revolutionize your communication and collaboration.

- **Microsoft SharePoint:** Discover how to organize and share resources effortlessly.

- **Microsoft OneDrive:** Simplify file management and access from anywhere.

- **Microsoft Copilot:** Let AI handle repetitive tasks across multiple apps.

Each app complements the others, creating an ecosystem that grows with you.

Think back to Sarah's story. Her journey wasn't just about learning new features—it was about changing her mindset. She went from feeling overwhelmed to empowered, from reactive to proactive.

Like Sarah, you've embarked on a journey of transformation. Every email you organize, every calendar event you schedule, and every task you prioritize is a step toward mastering your tools and reclaiming your time.

Continue reflecting on your progress and refining your workflow. The small adjustments you make today will pay off in big ways tomorrow.

This book is part of *The Microsoft 365 Companion Series*, designed to help you unlock the potential of tools like Outlook, Teams, SharePoint, OneDrive, and more. Each book is a standalone guide to mastering a specific app, but together, they form a comprehensive roadmap to becoming a Microsoft 365 expert.

Whether you're just starting out or looking to deepen your knowledge, there's a book in the series to meet you where you are.

The modern world is complex, but with the right tools and mindset, you can navigate it with confidence. Microsoft Outlook isn't just a tool—it's a partner in your success. By embracing its features and integrating it into your daily life, you're setting yourself up for greater productivity, clearer communication, and a more organized future.

So, where do you go from here? The answer is simple: keep learning, keep growing, and keep exploring. The journey you've started with Outlook is just the beginning. The tools are in your hands—now it's up to you to use them to create, collaborate, and thrive.

The future of your productivity is bright. Let's embrace it together.